TRY NOT TO LAUGH CHALLENGE

DAD JOKE EDITION

Howling
Moon Books

Published in 2018 by
Howling Moon Books

Printed in the United States of America

ALSO FROM
HOWLING MOON BOOKS:

Try Not to Laugh Challenge!
Dad Joke Edition
Rules:

Pick your team, or go one on one.

Sit across from each other & make eye contact.

Take turns reading jokes to each other.

You can make silly faces, funny voices & sound effects to get your opponents to laugh more.

When your opponent laughs, you get a point!

First team to get 3 points, wins!

If you're laughing, you're losing!

WARNING!
THIS JOKE BOOK IS ARMED & DADLY!

IF YOUR KIDS ARE IMMUNE TO DAD JOKES, DON'T FRET!

TRY ONE OF THREE CHALLENGES AGAINST THEM!

NORMAL MODE:
TRY NOT TO LAUGH

PUN-ISHMENT MODE:
TRY NOT TO ROLL YOUR EYES

DADLY MODE:
TRY NOT TO GROAN

NOW, LETTUCE BEGIN THE PUN-ISHMENT!

I'll give you my best Dad Joke.

But you have to promise
to give it back!

What did the horse say
when it fell?

Help I've fallen and
I can't giddy-up!

Why wouldn't the bike stand
up by itself?

It was two tired.

I'm only familiar with 25 letters
of the alphabet.

I don't know y.

KID:

Dad, can you put my shoes on?

DAD:

Sorry kid, I don't think they'll fit me.

Why did the Dad carry two
pairs of pants while he golfed?

In case he got a hole in one.

Why do people at buffets
look stressed?

Because they have a
lot on their plate.

What do you call a man with no arms, or legs in the middle of the ocean?

Bob.

I used to be addicted to the Hokey Pokey, but then I turned myself around.

(DAUGHTER STUBS HER TOE)

DAD:
Quick! Call Whine – 1–1 we need a whambulence!

DAUGHTER:
Ow! No, Dad!

DAD:
Want me to call a toe truck at least?

Why shouldn't you
DAB backwards?

Because that would
be BAD.

When is a door not a door?

When it's ajar.

How do you feel after you
eat too much?

All full.

What does a cop do after
a big chase?

He takes a-rest.

Have you heard of
that Top Secret bakery?

I didn't think so, it's
on a knead to dough basis.

What do you call a cow
in an earthquake?

Milkshake

Why did the old man
fall down the well?

Because he couldn't
see that well.

What did the plant say to the
hungry caterpillars all over it?

LEAF ME ALONE.

How do you make an egg roll?

You push it.

What does a clock do when
it's hungry?

It goes back four seconds.

Knock Knock.
Who's there?
Water.
Water who?
Water you doing in my house?

Knock knock.
Who's there?
Justin.
Justin who?
Justin time! I thought you
weren't home.

What is a kid guilty of
when they won't take a nap?

Resisting a rest.

I just burned 2,000 calories!

That's the last time I'll leave
brownies in the oven while I nap.

What do you suffer from if you are a Marathoner who wears bad shoes?

Agony of de feet.

What do you call a dinosaur that lost his glasses?

Doyouthinkhesaurus.

WAITRESS:

Careful, the plate is hot!

DAD:

It's okay, I'm not attracted to plates.

A man tried to sell
me a coffin today.

I told him that was
the last thing I need.

How long does it take
to make butter?

An e-churnity.

A weasel walks into a bar.
The bartender looks up and
says, "Wow! In all my years,
I've never had a weasel stop by.
What can I get you?"
"Pop" goes the weasel.

What do cows like to read?

Cattle logs.

What do you call a
deer with no eyes?

No ideer.

What do you call a deer
with no eyes and no legs?

Still no ideer.

100 Years ago rich people had
cars and poor people had horses.
Now only rich people have
horses and poor people have cars.

My how the stables have turned.

My dad named our dogs
Rolex and Timex.

Because they're our
watch dogs.

Why did the corn
start crying?

Because the farmer
ripped its ears off.

Why did the chicken
cross the playground?

To get to the other slide!

I got a parking ticket the other day, and I don't understand why.

The sign clearly said, "Fine For Parking".

Thank you student loans
for getting my kids
through college.
I don't think I can ever
repay you.

(Dad looks at the hole in his sock)

Why was the Koala let
into the science lab?

Because he was
totally Koala-fied.

What do gardeners sing
when they're planting seeds?

Thistle while you work.

Knock Knock.
Who's there?
Dishes.
Dishes who?
Dishes a nice place you got here.

Knock knock.
Who's there?
Dwayne.
Dwayne who?
Dwayne the bathtub,
I'm dwowning.

What did the seamstress
say when she finished
her work?

I'm sew done.

What is an artist's
favorite Disney song?

Let it Gogh!

What did the Dad Spider
tell his child?

"You spend too much
time on the web."

I had a joke to tell you,
but then I thought,
tree jokes are too sappy.

What do you call a swimming
pool when your whole
family is in it?

A gene pool.

Humpty Dumpty always seems
to have terrible summers.

But at least he had a great Fall.

Singing in the shower is all
fun and games until you get
shampoo in your mouth.

Then it becomes a soap opera.

Why can't you have a
nose 12 inches long?

Because then it would
be a foot.

Knock Knock.
Who's there?
Isabel.
Isabel who?
Isabel working? I had to knock.

Knock knock.
Who's there?
Radio.
Radio who?
Radio not. Here I come.

(Waitress hands Dad the check)

DAD:

I didn't order that.

WAITRESS:

It comes free with the meal!

What did the buffalo tell his
kid when he dropped
him off at school?

Bison.

You can't plant any flowers
if you haven't botany.

What do you call an owl
who sleeps with one eye open?

The Owl seeing eye

What did the corn field tell
the scarecrow when he
needed to talk?

We're all ears.

Astronomers got tired
after watching the moon go
around the earth for 24 hours,
so they decided to call it a day.

Why do crows only get
hit by trucks?

Because the lookout Crow can
only tell them when a
"CAW" is coming.

DAUGHTER:

Why doesn't swordfish flake apart like other fish?

DAD:

I don't know, I guess it's that sword-of-fish.

What did the bird say to the
other birds when he
saw a cat?

Fly, you fools!

What do you call a bear who
just woke up from hibernating?

Bearly awake.

Why do cows wear bells?

Because their horns don't work.

What is a fisherman's motto?

Keepin' it Reel.

I put Grandma on speed dial,
does that make her
an Insta-Gram?

Where does water
keep it's money?

At the River Bank

WAITRESS:

Do you wanna box for that?

DAD:

No, but I'll wrestle you for it!

Dad's cooking skills are so un-grill-ievable! I have never seen him make a mis-steak. I don't think I'll ever be able to ketchup.

What did the point shoes tell the ballerina?

"I'm just keeping you on your toes."

What do you call the
security guards outside
of Samsung stores?

Guardians of the Galaxy.

Whenever I try to eat healthy,
a chocolate bar looks at me
and Snickers.

Whoever invented the bandage
was a bloody genius!

What do you call a monkey that
wins the World Series?

A Chimpion

DAD:

I'll have a soda, please.

WAITRESS:

Would you like it in the can?

DAD:

No, I'll have it here.

I ordered a thesaurus,
and when it came in it was
all blank inside. I have no words
to describe how angry I am.

Why do we tell actors
to break a leg?

Because every show
needs a cast!

I took an underground train
to the sandwich shop today.

It was a Subway.

I don't think I need a spine,
it just holds me back.

(Doctor asking a series of standard questions to Dad)

DOCTOR:

Do you smoke?

DAD:

...only when I'm on fire.

With the rise of self-driving vehicles, it's only a matter of time before we have a country song where a guy's truck leaves him, too.

When does a joke become a Dad Joke?

When it's fully groan.

Knock Knock.
Who's there?
Ice Cream.
Ice Cream who?
Ice Cream if you don't let me in!

Knock, knock.
Who's there?
Wooden shoe.
Wooden shoe who?
Wooden shoe like to hear
another joke?

To the guy who invented
the zero, thanks for nothing!

What do you stand on when
you practice a speech in
the shower?

A soapbox.

What did the squirrel say
when its tail was cut off?

It won't be long now.

Did you know all ants
are actually females?

If they were male, they
would be called Uncles.

KID:

If you give me $20, I'll be good.

DAD:

When I was your age, I was good for nothing.

I have a condition that makes
me eat while I sleep, it's called
insom-nom-nom-nom-ia.

Who is your smallest relative?

Your ant.

Whenever someone
tells me, "C'est la vie",

I tell them, "la vie".

Some people think filling animals
with helium is wrong.

I say, hey whatever
floats your goat.

DAD:

Be careful standing next to those trees.

KID:

Why?

DAD:

I dunno, they just seem kinda shady to me.

Good steak puns are a rare
medium done well.

Women must find Dad jokes
attractive, otherwise they
would be called Bachelor jokes.

When does a joke become
a Dad joke?

When it becomes apparent.

I tried to teach my Dad how
to store his passwords on the
Cloud so he would always
have them. He turned to me
and asked, "But what if it's sunny?"

MOM:

Can you put the trash out?

DAD:

I didn't know it was on fire.

My Dad said I would never
amount to anything because
I procrastinate.

I told him, "Oh, yeah?
Just you wait!"

What is a Sea Monster's
favorite pastime?

Kraken Jokes!

Did you hear about the
kidnapping at school?

He woke up.

A Dad was washing the car with
his son. The son asks,
"Dad, can we please use a sponge!"

Knock Knock.
Who's there?
Thermos.
Thermos who?
Thermos be a better way of
getting through to you.

Knock knock.
Who's there?
Hatch.
Hatch who?
Gesundheit.

WAITRESS:

Soup or salad?

DAD:

I don't want a Super Salad, I just want a regular salad.

Which animal always wins
at poker?

A Cheetah.

What lies at the bottom
of the ocean and twitches?

A nervous wreck.

Vegetarians regret their
lifestyle because it's
all a missed steak.

Wanna hear a dirty joke?

A sloth fell in the mud.

Wanna hear a clean joke?

The muddy sloth got a bath.

MOM:

How do I look?

DAD:

With your eyes.

What did the baseball player
say when he was on third base?

There's no plate like home.

Which mountain finished school?

Mt. Cleverest.

What is the least spoken language
in the world?

Sign language.

Learning how to pick locks has
really opened a lot of
doors for me!

DAUGHTER:
Dad, why didn't I get sunburned on the beach?

DAD:
You can't get sunburned.

DAUGHTER:
Really?

DAD:
You can only get daughter-burned.

I went to the zoo yesterday
and saw a baguette in a cage.

The zoo keeper told me it
was bread in captivity.

I don't always tell Dad jokes,
but when I do, he laughs.

You gotta hand it
to short people,
cause they can't
reach it on their own.

Did you hear about
the circus in town?

I heard it was in tents.

KID:

Stop pretending
to be butter!

DAD:

But, I'm on a roll.

Why can't two elephants go
swimming at the same time?

Because they only have one
pair of trunks between them.

What do you call dental x-rays?

Tooth pics

How do panda's scare each other?

With Bam...BOO!

Who is Irish and always
sits on the lawn?

Paddy O'Furniture.

Knock Knock.
Who's there?
Razor.
Razor who?
Razor hands! This is a stick up!

Knock knock.
Who's there?
Interrupting cow.
Interrupting c—?
MOO!

What does a Dad say when
a bug hits the windshield?

DAD:

I bet he doesn't
have the guts to
do that again!

When does a courtroom
smell good?

When it is full of judge-mint.

A pizza walks into a bar.
The bartender says,
"Sorry, we don't serve food here."

I'm reading a book on antigravity.

It's impossible to put down!

Spring is here! I'm so happy,
I wet my plants.

CASHIER:

Would you like the milk in a bag?

DAD:

No, leave it in the carton.

What sound does a 747 make
when it bounces?

Boeing, Boeing, Boeing!

Did you know they made round
hay bails illegal?

Apparently cows weren't
getting a square meal.

Do you think that people
who climb Mt. Everest,
ever rest?

What happened after the
invention of the wheel?

A revolution.

When do you buy a boat?

When it's on sail.

What type of metal enforces
the law?

Copper

KID:
Dad, you're not even listening to me.

DAD:
That's a weird way to start a conversation.

Why are pigs so bad
at soccer?

They are always hogging
the ball.

Two guys walk into a bar,
the third one ducks.

Have you ever thought
about living in a fungus?

There's so mushroom!

My friend keeps telling me,
"Cheer up! It could be worse,
you could be stuck underground
in a hole full of water."

I know he means, well.

What would bears be
without bees?

Ears

The plural of penny is pence. But
we say pennies because it
makes more scents!

Why didn't the tomatoes want
to be planted next to the corn?

Because the corn was
a bit of a stalker.

What do you call a
happy cowboy?

A jolly rancher.

Knock Knock.
Who's there?
Voodoo.
Voodoo who?
Voodoo you think you are, asking
me so many questions?

Knock, knock.
Who's there?
Alien
Alien who?
Just how many aliens do you know?

MOM:

Did you get a haircut?

DAD:

No, I got them all cut.

Why is the ocean so salty?

Because the land doesn't
wave back.

I can always tell just by looking
when someone is lying.

I can also tell when
they're standing.

What do you call a cat that catches mice?

Expurrminator.

Why are Dalmatians bad at hide and seek?

Because they're always spotted!

What is the worst thing about
Ancient History teachers?

They tend to Babylon.

How did the tree feel when
Spring began?

Re-leaved!

SON:

I'm hungry.

DAD:

Hi, Hungry! I'm Dad...
I don't remember
calling you "Hungry".

SON:

Dad, I'm serious!

DAD:

Serious? I thought
you said you were
Hungry?

Why can't you tell your
secrets to a clock?

Cause time will tell.

Which bird always has
a song stuck in it's head?

A hummingbird.

I would tell you a pizza joke,
but it's a little cheesy.

Which country has the fastest
growing capital city?

Ireland, every year
it's Dublin.

What is a Plummer's favorite
kind of shoes?

Clogs

If I get a horse,
I'm going to call him Mayo.

Because Mayo neighs.

(Dad playing a video game)

KID:

Dad, can you help me with my homework?

DAD:

Sorry, I've got my hands full right now.

When I get a dog, I'm going to name him Five Miles. Then I can tell everyone I walk Five Miles, everyday.

Want to hear something terrible?

Paper.
See? I told you it was tear-able.

Why do unicorns sleep in late?

Because they don't believe
in mornings.

What is a sheep's
favorite band?

Ewe2

When I was told to
stop impersonating a flamingo,
I had to put my foot down.

What's the best thing about
elevator jokes?

They work on so many levels.

(On the First day of Spring)

DAD:

Have you herb?

KID:

What?

DAD:

It's thyme to plant!

What kind of ice cream
does a Deer eat?

Cookie Doe

What do you call a dog in
an underwater vessel?

Scuba Doo

Knock Knock.
Who's there?
A little old lady.
A little old lady who?
All this time, I didn't know
you could yodel!

Knock, knock.
Who's there?
Comb
Comb who?
Comb on down and I'll tell you!

What does a thesaurus eat
for breakfast?

A synonym roll.

I once offered a teddy
bear dinner. But he said,
"No, thanks. I'm already stuffed."

DAD:

Want to hear a whale joke, it's a real Killer.

KID:

Dad, why are you pun-ishing me?

DAD:

...I'm not doing it on porpoise.

What position does a cat
play in baseball?

Cat-cher

Why didn't the toilet paper
cross the road?

It got stuck in a crack.

How do you keep intruders out
of a castle made of cheese?

Moatzarella

What do Realestate
agents drink?

Proper Tea.

KID:

Dad, do you know the difference between a pack of wolves and a pack of cookies?

DAD:

No. What?

KID:

It's a good thing Mom does the grocery shopping then.

Did you know you don't need
a class to train garbage men?

They just pick it up as
they go along.

What did the DJ
say to the Farmer?

Lettuce Turnip the Beet

A clown once held a door
open for me.

I thought it was a nice jester.

What do you call an
average potato?

A commentator.

DAD:
Can I have a
Root Beer?

WAITRESS:
Sorry, we don't have
Root Beer. What
about Ginger ale?

DAD:
That's soda
close, but no. I'll
just have water.

What do you call a situation where your sister is in tears?

A Cry Sis

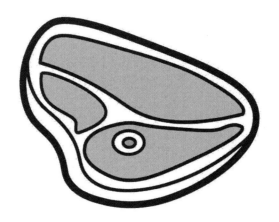

What's the difference between a poorly dressed person on a unicycle and a well dressed person on a bicycle?

Attire.

Whoever invented the knock-knock joke should get the no bell prize.

It's hard to explain puns to Kleptomaniacs.

They always take things, literally.

MOM:

Can you call me a taxi?

DAD:

Okay, you're a taxi!

What did the ice cube say to
the glass of water?

I was water before it got cool.

What do you call a criminal that
was caught in a cornfield?

Cornered.

Knock Knock.
Who's there?
Cow says.
Cow says who?
No. Cow says MOOOOO!

Knock, knock.
Who's there?
Kenya
Kenya who?
Kenya guess who is it?

DAD:

I'll have some bacon and eggs, please.

WAITRESS:

How do you like your eggs?

DAD:

I don't know, I haven't had them yet.

Why was the archaeologist sad?

Because his whole life
was in ruins.

A man just assaulted me with
milk, cheese and yogurt.

How dairy.

What did the golfing caterpillar
grow up to be?

A putter-fly

Why do trees hate tests?

Because the questions
always stump them.

(Dad Driving)

DAD:

Look kids, a flock of cows!

KIDS:

Herd of cows, Dad.

DAD:

Of course I've heard of cows, there's a flock of them over there!

What did the baby corn
say to the mama corn?

Where's the pop corn?

Mom hates when I hide
the kitchen utensils,
but that's a whisk
I am willing to take.

Knock Knock.
Who's there?
Otis.
Otis who?
Otis is a wonderful way to
treat your Dad.

Knock, knock.
Who's there?
Spell.
Spell who?
W-H-O

Where should you never
take a dog?

To the flea market.

Did you hear about the cheese
factory that burned down?

There was nothing left
but da Brie.

What do you call a
citrus submarine?

Sub-lime

What should you say when you
are in the mood for
Japanese soup?

Miso hungry.

DAD:
Let me see your report card.

SON:
I don't have it right now.

DAD:
Why not?

SON:
My friend is borrowing it, he wants to scare his parents.

Why should you always lean
over your plate when you
eat lasagna?

Because you'll get less-on-ya.

Which rock group has four
men what don't sing?

Mount Rushmore.

Where is happiness made?

At the satisfactory.

What do you call a nocturnal blood sucking insect?

A Luna Tick

What do crows drink
in the morning?

CAW-fee

Don't spell part backwards.

It's a trap!

What does a Dad say when he puts a car in reverse?

DAD:

This really takes me back.

Why are teen girls always
at odds?

Because they can't even.

I have a fear of speed bumps.

But I'm slowly getting over it.

How to you make a gold soup?

You put 24 carrots in it.

Where should you buy water?

At a liquidation sale.

SON:

Are bugs good to eat, Dad?

DAD:

Not at the dinner table. Ask me later.

-------ONE MEAL LATER-------

DAD:

What did you want to know about eating bugs?

SON:

Nevermind. There was a bug in your soup. But now it's gone.

What did the fisherman say
to the magician?

Pick a Cod, any Cod.

What happens when
you run out of crackers?

You're cracka lackin'

Man, this Tuesday is dragging on so long it's starting to feel like Threesday.

What happened when the escalator broke down?

Everyone stopped and staired.

What's in the wardrobe?

Narnia business.

What do you call it when
a cow wrongs you?

Pure and utter betrayal.

What is the richest fish
in the world?

A Goldfish

What do runners do when
they forget something?

They jog their memory.

SON:

I'll call you later.

DAD:

Don't call me later,
call me Dad.

How do you split Rome in half?

You use a pair of Caesars!

Why do dolphins swim
in salt water?

Because if they swam in pepper
water, they would sneeze.

Why did the skeleton cancel
his skull-pture gallery opening?

Because his heart wasn't in it.

What is the best part
about living in Switzerland?

I don't know,
but the flag is a big plus!

What is a vegetable's
favorite kind of music?

Broc n' Roll

What do vets say when a
dog swallows a wedding ring?

There's a diamond in the ruff.

Made in the USA
Columbia, SC
09 June 2019